MATERIALS ALL AROUND US

MATERIALS TECHNOLOGY

Robert Snedden

Heinemann
LIBRARY

H www.heinemann.co.uk/library
Visit our website to find out more information about Heinemann Library books.

To order:
☎ Phone 44 (0) 1865 888066
📄 Send a fax to 44 (0) 1865 314091
💻 Visit the Heinemann Bookshop at www.heinemann.co.uk/library to browse our catalogue and order online.

First published in Great Britain by Heinemann Library,
Halley Court, Jordan Hill, Oxford OX2 8EJ
a division of Reed Educational and Professional Publishing Ltd.
Heinemann is a registered trademark of Reed Educational & Professional
Publishing Ltd.

OXFORD MELBOURNE AUCKLAND
JOHANNESBURG BLANTYRE GABORONE
IBADAN PORTSMOUTH (NH) USA CHICAGO

Designed by Celia Floyd
Originated by Dot Gradations
Printed by Wing King Tong, Hong Kong

ISBN 0 431 12093 5
05 04 03 02 01
10 9 8 7 6 5 4 3 2 1

British Library Cataloguing in Publication Data

Snedden, Robert
  Materials technology. – (Material all around us)
  1.Materials science - Juvenile literature
  I.Title
  620.1'1

Acknowledgements
The Publishers would like to thank the following for permission to reproduce
photographs: Ancient Art and Architecture: p13; Andrew Lambert: p21; FLPA: B
Borrell p4; Nutan/Rapho/Network p11; Sally and Richard Greenhill: p14; Science
Photo Library: Martyn F Chillmaid p6, Martin Bond p8, David Parker p9, Chris
Knapton p15, Harvey Pincis p16, Maximilian Stock p17, James Stevenson p18, Tek
Image p19, James Holmes/Thompson Laboratories p24, NASA pp26, 27, Peter
Menzel p29; Tony Stone Images: Chris Shinn p5, Ross Harrison Koty p12, Keith
Wood p23, Wayne Eastep p25

Cover photograph reproduced with permission of Science Photo Library

Every effort has been made to contact copyright holders of any material
reproduced in this book. Any omissions will be rectified in subsequent printings if
notice is given to the Publisher.

Any words appearing in the text in bold, **like this**, are explained in the glossary.

Contents

Using materials

Materials are used for making things. Natural materials such as stone, wood and wool can be used more or less as they are. Perhaps we might just need to clean and shape them. Other materials, such as plastics, have to be made first or, like metals, have to be separated out from less useful substances.

Materials that have been used for a long time may still be made in the same way. The way we make concrete is not so different from the way the Ancient Romans made it. New materials may be produced by careful work or sometimes even by accident.

Different materials are good for doing different things. The trick is in deciding which material is best for a particular job. Copper wires are good at conducting electricity but probably uncomfortable knitted into a jumper.

Materials like wood require little processing other than cutting into the desired shape.

Extracting the materials we need from the ground often has undesirable effects such as damage to the landscape.

On the other hand sheep's wool makes a warm jumper but is rather poor at conducting electricity!

Science and materials

Some differences between materials are obvious, such as the fact that wood floats but rocks do not. Other differences might not be so easy to spot. A materials scientist looks at the way materials are put together to work out how and why they behave as they do. The job of a materials engineer is to find new and improved ways of using existing materials or to find ways of making new materials. The scientists and the engineers work together to produce the huge range of materials that we use every day.

One thing is certain – the job of a materials scientist will never be done because we will always want to make new things.

The right materials for the job

Matching the material to the job it has to do is hugely important. It would be terrible if a bridge collapsed because the builders had used the wrong materials, for example. To do this we need to know what properties the material has.

Properties of materials

The properties of materials can be divided into different groups.

1 Mechanical properties

Mechanics deal with objects in motion and the forces acting on them. Mechanical properties are important in a wide variety of structures and objects, ranging from guitar strings to rocket engines. Some of the most important mechanical properties of materials are:

stiffness – how much a material will bend

Stress tests are carried out to see how well a material will stand up to the demands placed on it.

resistance to **stress** – how much a material can be stretched or squashed
toughness – how much a material can resist cracking
strength – how much force it takes to break a material.

2 Chemical properties

The chemical properties of a material tell us how resistant it is to attack by **acids** and other chemicals that might damage it.

3 Electrical properties

Electrical properties tell us whether or not a material will conduct electricity. This is important in deciding whether to use the material as a **conductor** or as an **insulator**.

Try it yourself

You will need
a selection of everyday items such as a piece of wood, an old plate, an empty tin, a piece of brick, an empty plastic drinks bottle (please check with an adult before using these items)
a chopping board
a cloth
a hammer

SAFETY: Always have an adult to supervise this activity

1 Put an item on the chopping board and cover it with the cloth.
   WARNING: always cover the item with a cloth in order to protect your eyes!

2 Give the item a sharp blow with the hammer. What happens to it? Does it bend or break? Does it crack? Does it resist the blow entirely? Try this with all your items.

Superconductors

Some materials are better at conducting electricity than others. No materials, not even metals, let electricity pass through without some of the electrical energy being lost.

However, if some materials are cooled to very very low temperatures, their **resistance** to electricity drops to nearly zero. We call these materials **superconductors**.

Pollution-free high-speed trains could speed through the countryside using magnetic fields generated by super-conductors.

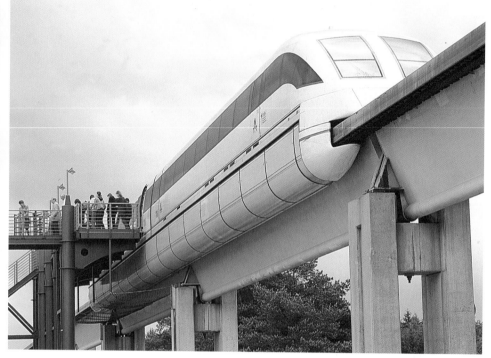

The first superconductor

Superconducting was first discovered in the Netherlands in 1911 by Heike Kamerlingh-Onnes. He was studying the properties of materials at very low temperatures. When he cooled mercury to a temperature of ⁻269°C he found its resistance to electricity vanished.

It just keeps going and going and ...

Scientists in the United States connected batteries to a superconductor to make a **current** flow. Then they removed the batteries, but the current kept right on flowing as if the batteries were still in place. It was still flowing four years later when the scientists finally dismantled the circuit.

Everyday superconductors

Until scientists can find a way to make superconductors that work at closer to everyday temperatures their properties will only be seen in the laboratory. The hope is to produce superconductors that can be kept cool enough to work cheaply and easily.

Electricity flowing through superconducting cables could reach homes and industries without loss of energy. Computers with superconducting components would be faster and more powerful than any we have today.

A magnet floats above this superconducting disc. A magnetic field is generated by the disc when it becomes superconducting.

Polymers

A **polymer** is a substance that is made by joining a great many identical small **molecules** together to make a long chain. The small molecules are called **monomers** and there may be many thousands in a polymer chain.

You probably come across polymers everyday. Starch, found in many foods such as potatoes and rice, is a natural polymer. Plants make it by linking together many sugar molecules to make a food store.

This form of polymerization is called condensation polymerization because water is produced as the monomers join together.

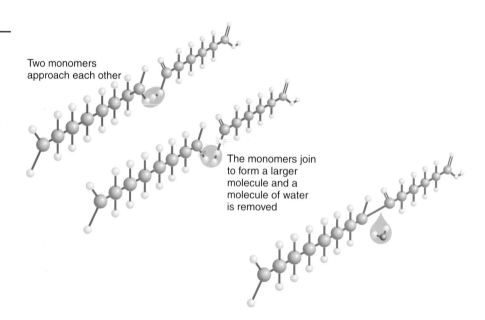

Two monomers approach each other

The monomers join to form a larger molecule and a molecule of water is removed

Synthetic polymers

The first synthetic polymer was bakelite, a brittle form of plastic, which was made in the United States in 1909 by Leo Hendrick Baekeland. The first polymer to be made entirely from chemicals was nylon, which was developed in the 1930s. Polyethylene, a tough plastic with many uses, is also an example of a polymer that was created in the laboratory.

Polymer properties

The great length of a polymer molecule gives it some useful properties. Polymers do not dissolve easily because the molecules are so big. Rubber is a polymer that is found naturally and can also be made in the laboratory. It can be stretched to many times its original length because the polymer chains simply straighten out as it is pulled and then curl back up again when it is released.

Polymers are used in making fibreglass for boat hulls.

Alloys

Many metals are too soft to be useful. However, they can be made more useful by mixing them with other materials to produce **alloys**. An alloy usually contains a large amount of one metal, called the base metal. To this are added smaller amounts of other materials. These can be other metals or non-metals such as carbon and silicon. Alloys are usually made by melting the base metal and then adding the other materials to it.

Alloy properties

Alloys are stronger and harder than pure metals. However, they are more difficult to hammer into shape, to draw into wires, or roll into sheets. Most alloys have a lower melting point that pure metals.

12

Some alloys and their uses

Aluminium alloy is as strong as steel and only slightly heavier than pure aluminium. It is used when a metal that is strong but light is needed, for example for drinks cans and bicycle parts.

Magnesium alloys are used for making aircraft and car parts.

Titanium alloys are very strong and light. They are used to make jet engines and tough, resistant equipment for chemical plants.

Iron and steel

Iron is almost always used as an alloy, most often in the form of steel. Two common steel alloys are:
- Carbon steels are the most widely used steels. They are strong and **durable** and used in buildings, in car manufacture and for food storage.
- Stainless steels resist **corrosion** very well and are used to make medical equipment and kitchen utensils.

The first alloys

The first alloy ever made was bronze which is made using copper as a base metal. It was produced accidentally around 5500 years ago. Bronze is copper mixed with tin. It is much harder than pure copper and was used to make tools and weapons.

Bronze was the first alloy to be discovered and was soon being used to make tools and weapons.

Ceramics

Ceramics are materials that need high temperatures to be made. Most ceramics are hard and resistant to heat and chemicals. They include everyday materials such as bricks, cement and glass and more unusual materials such as rocket nose cones.

Making ceramics

1 Clays and other materials used to make ceramics are dug from the earth.
2 Impurities are removed and then the materials are crushed and ground into fine **particles**.
3 The correct amounts of each are mixed together and water or some other liquid is added. The mixture can then be formed into whatever shape is wanted.
4 After the ceramic has been shaped it is left to dry.
5 Next it is strengthened by firing. This means placing it in a special **furnace** called a kiln. Firing hardens the ceramic and gives it strength and **durability**.

Ceramics are fired in furnaces called kilns like this one.

Glass and some heat resistant ceramics are made by melting the particles and then shaping them. Many ceramic products are covered with a glassy coating called a glaze. This gives the ceramic a smoother surface and makes it waterproof.

*Electricity does not pass through ceramics so they are used as **insulators** in electrical equipment and on power lines. Heat resistant ceramics are used in furnaces that produce steel. Ceramic tiles protect a space shuttle from the intense heat as it re-enters the Earth's atmosphere.*

Ceramics are often used as insulators on high **voltage** power lines.

Ceramic products

Some extremely hard ceramics are used for cutting metals and for grinding, polishing and sanding various surfaces. Clay and shale are used to make strong hard wearing bricks and drainpipes. Baths, sinks and toilets are often made from porcelain, which is a ceramic. Ceramics make excellent containers for foods and drinks because they are resistant to chemicals, do not absorb liquids and can withstand sudden changes in temperature.

Common ceramics such as porcelain are poor conductors of electricity and this property makes them good insulators. They are used as insulators in spark plugs, on electricity power lines and in electrical equipment such as television sets.

Glass

It is hard to imagine life without glass. It is used to make containers for storing drinks and other containers, called glasses, from which to drink them. It is used to make lenses for telescopes, microscopes and for spectacles. Light comes into our homes, schools and work places through glass windows.

Glass is a first-class storage material; easy to make, unreactive and clear so you can see what's inside!

Making glass

No one knows when or where people first learned how to make glass. The first manufactured glass is believed to have been a glaze on ceramic vessels, some time in the 3000s BC.

*A large amount of silica sand and small amounts of soda ash and limestone are mixed together. Other materials may be added to give the glass special qualities. The mixture is heated in a **furnace** until it forms a syrupy mass. When it is allowed to cool it forms glass.*

Types of glass

There are many different kinds of glass, with different uses. Here are just a few of them.

Glass-ceramics

These are very strong. They are resistant to chemicals, can withstand high temperatures and sudden changes in temperature. They have a wide range of uses, from cookware to the nose cones of guided missiles.

Laminated safety glass

This is made from layers of plastic material and flat glass. If something strikes the outside glass layer and breaks it, the inner plastic layer stretches and holds the broken pieces of glass together, stopping them from flying in all directions. Car windscreens are made from laminated glass.

Tempered safety glass

This looks like ordinary glass but it is given a special heat treatment and can be five times as strong. Even a blow from a hammer won't break it. If it does break, it collapses into small, dull-edged fragments. It is often used for shop doors.

Grinding a telescope lens takes patience and skill to make sure it has no flaws.

Fibreglass

Each **fibre** is a very thin rod of solid glass. Glass fibres can be used to make fire-resistant glass cloth. Thin, extremely pure optical fibres can transmit telephone and television signals over long distances.

The chemical industry

It is the job of the chemical industry to take **raw materials** such as oil and gas from the world around us and transform them into useful materials that can be put to work for a variety of different purposes.

In a chemical plant raw materials are made into useful products on a large scale.

Paper, glass, metal **alloys**, plastics and synthetic **fibres** are all made by the chemical industry.

The industry also provides a tremendous variety of raw materials to be used in the manufacture of other products. Sulphuric acid, for example, is used to produce **fertilizers**, paints, explosives and many other chemicals.

Chemical engineers

Chemical engineers deal with the chemical processes that change raw materials into useful products.

They plan, design, and help to construct **chemical plants** and equipment. They develop efficient and economical ways of producing chemicals such as cosmetics, soaps, drugs, explosives, fertilizers, food additives, fuels and plastics.

Try it out for size

Chemical engineers will construct miniature scale models of a new chemical plant and run checks on the various processes that will be carried out in the full-size plant. Once they are sure that there are no safety risks the building work can begin. This can save a lot of time and money.

The choice of a place to build is also important. The raw materials needed for the chemical process need to be readily available. The finished products have to be transported quickly to where they are needed. Both of these things have to be taken into account to keep costs down.

Many of the materials and products of the chemical industry are highly dangerous if they are not handled carefully.

Materials and food

Many different materials are used in the production and storage of food. Chemicals are used to preserve it, metal, paper and plastics are used for storage, additives such as colourings and flavourings are used to make food look and taste more appealing.

Preservatives

One of the oldest methods of food preservation is curing. This involves adding ingredients such as salt, spices and sugar to food. They may be rubbed on to the food or the food may be soaked in a **solution** of the ingredients. It is often used to preserve meat products as well as fish, potatoes, cucumbers and some nuts. Some meat and fish are cured by smoking. Wood smoke contains chemicals that slow the growth of bacteria.

Canning

Canning involves foods being sealed in airtight containers and then heated to destroy bacteria that may cause spoilage. A wide variety of foods can be preserved in this way.

Canning food can help to preserve it for a longer period of time.

One of the disadvantages of canning is that the heating changes the food's texture, colour and flavour. Some **nutrients** are lost in the canning process too. Often additives may be added to put some of these things back.

Additives

Additives are chemicals that are added to foods to prevent spoilage, improve appearance or to increase nutrients. There are hundreds of different additives. Some help keep foods edible for as long as possible. Flavouring agents can be natural, such as spices and fruit juices, as well as artificial flavour enhancers, such as monosodium glutamate (MSG).

Empty the contents of one sachet into a cup or mug, add ⅓ pint (190 ml) of boiling water and stir well.

INGREDIENTS: DRIED GLUCOSE SYRUP, MODIFIED STARCH, DRIED SWEETCORN, VEGETABLE FAT, SALT, FLAVOUR ENHANCERS: MONOSODIUM GLUTAMATE, SODIUM '5' RIBONUCLEOTIDES; DRIED CHICKEN, HYDROLYSED VEGETABLE PROTEIN, FLAVOURINGS, CASEINATE, DRIED ONION, DRIED TOMATO, ACIDITY REGULATOR: E340; EMULSIFIERS: E471, E472(b); STABILISER: E412; HERBS, COLOUR: E160(b); SPICES, ANTIOXIDANT: E320

31 gram **1.1** oz per twin pack

Oranger oranges

Colouring agents are often added to make foods look appealing. Orange colouring agents are often added to the skins of oranges to improve their appearance. Colouring agents are used a lot in the manufacture of sweets.

You can see what additives are in food products by looking at the ingredients label.

Medical materials

A prosthesis is an artificial part that does the job of a body part. The body part may have been lost or damaged as the result of injury, disease or a birth defect. Some types of prostheses are used inside the body. For example, damaged hip joints can be replaced by artificial ones made of metal and plastic. Metal pins are used to help broken bones heal. Artificial heart valves can be used to help people with heart problems. Some mechanical devices are used to do the job of a body part without actually replacing it, such as a pacemaker that keeps the beating of the heart steady.

Although artificial limbs are not as good as the real thing they are of great benefit to many people.

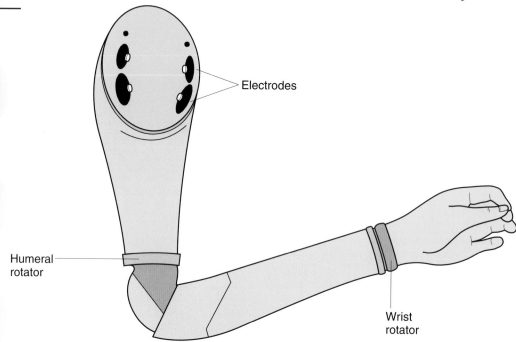

Electrodes

Humeral rotator

Wrist rotator

Biomedical engineers

Biomedical engineers use their skills and knowledge to solve problems in biology and medicine. They design medical instruments for monitoring, diagnosing and treating diseases. They also test different materials to find which are best for use as artificial body parts. Engineers have helped with inventions such as replacement heart valves and the artificial kidney.

The right materials

A replacement body part should ideally last a lifetime. Selecting the right materials to place inside the human body is a very important task. It is vital that the new material should cause no harmful effects in the body. At the same time the body's defences should do no damage to the new material that might stop it from doing its job. Suitable materials include certain **ceramics**, metal **alloys** and plastics.

Medicines

Several important medicines are obtained from plants and **moulds**. The **antibiotic** penicillin comes from a mould, for example. Some common drugs are made from **minerals**. Researchers are continually looking for new and more effective drugs. They may find a new drug from a natural source or they might make a new chemical **compound** in the laboratory.

Chemists carry out tests on a variety of materials in the search for new medicines.

Materials on the farm

A well-watered, fertile soil usually supplies all the **nutrients** and water that plants need to grow. However, if many plants are grown together the amount of nutrients and water they require for healthy growth may be greater than nature alone can provide. Most crops need large amounts of nitrogen, phosphorus and potassium, but chemical companies can provide **fertilizers** for almost any type of crop. Farmers can send samples of their soil to a soil-testing laboratory to learn which nutrients may need to be added.

Pesticides

Most farmers control pests with chemicals called **pesticides**. Chemists have developed hundreds of pesticides, each one designed to combat a certain type of weed, plant disease, or harmful insect. Pesticides are dangerous if they are used wrongly. They can do harm to animals and plants other than pests, or get into the food supply and so be a danger to humans too. For these reasons they must be used very carefully.

Farmers can send samples of soil to the laboratory for testing to discover if it is low in any nutrients.

Organic farming

Organic farmers use natural materials to fertilize soil and control pests. Manure is the most widely used organic fertilizer. It is readily available on farms that raise livestock. However, most crop farms have too few animals to produce the fertilizer their plants need.

Many farmers spray their crops with pesticides to kill insects – there is always a risk that these chemicals will harm other animals as well.

Try it yourself

You will need
moist gardening sand
two seed trays
plant fertilizer
some seeds, such as broad beans

1 Fill each tray with 3 or 4cm of sand. Add a little fertilizer to the sand in one of the trays.
2 Plant a few seeds in each tray making sure they are well covered.
3 Put the trays in a warm, well-lit place. Be sure to check the trays often and keep them moist.
4 After a few days the seeds should sprout into seedlings. Watch how they grow. Do you see any difference between the seedlings growing in the sand and those grown with fertilizer?

Materials in space

The materials used for building spacecraft and satellites have to be chosen very carefully. Weight is an important consideration. The heavier the craft the more fuel it will need to get into space and so the more expensive it will be to launch it. Panels of aluminium metal **alloy** are often used because these give great strength but weigh relatively little.

Materials used in space often need to last a long time too. A satellite might be working for thirty years and it would be tricky to send someone to replace a worn out part! As a satellite moves in and out of the sunlight as it orbits the Earth, the temperature changes from baking hot to freezing cold. Spacecraft designers have to know how much the materials used will expand and contract as they are heated and then cooled again. Protective materials can reflect heat away from parts of the spacecraft facing the sun while at the same time storing heat to prevent parts pointing away from the sun from getting too cold.

Building space stations in orbit around the Earth requires the use of many lightweight and durable materials.

Alloys in space

Materials scientists are developing many new alloys that provide greater strength and **durability** than ever before. These superalloys are made from the metals nickel or cobalt. They can resist extremely high temperatures and will be used in high performance jet aircraft as well as in spacecraft construction.

Space scientists are already planning to send an unmanned probe to an asteroid that will bring a rock sample back to Earth.

Space mining

One day we might get materials from space. Many asteroids are thought to contain water ice. The hydrogen and oxygen used to make rocket fuel could be obtained from that water. Some asteroids also have huge amounts of pure iron, nickel, cobalt, platinum and even gold. Even the smallest known asteroid of this kind could supply several times more metal than has been mined in all of human history.

Micromaterials

Some people believe that one day microscopic robots, able to push **atoms** and **molecules** together, could be used to produce a wide range of essential materials. Huge numbers of these nanorobots, as they are called, would supply materials at almost no cost, wiping out hunger and ending pollution from conventional factories.

What is nanotechnology?

Nanotechnology takes it name from the nanometre, which is one billionth of a metre (about three or four atoms wide). It means building things one atom or molecule at a time, placing them exactly where we want them. Nanotechnology could be used to produce materials of astonishing perfection, such as completely flawless metals that would be much stronger than anything we have today. It could mean supercomputers too small to see with the naked eye and spacecraft that were no more expensive to build than family cars.

A molecular machine – you!

If you want to see a nanotechnology machine right now, just look in the mirror. If you eat a banana, or anything else, chemicals in your body called proteins take it apart.

Smart materials

Imagine if you could simply touch the walls of your room and tell the smart nano-liquid covering them to produce a rainbow of colours, patterns and pictures until you found one you liked. The nano-liquid could be laced with nano-computers. Your whole room could be a videoscreen.

Some of the food is used for energy and some of it is reassembled as parts of you. Scientists have begun to design proteins in the laboratory that can perform particular tasks.

Will it ever happen?

Some nanotechnologists believe that these wonderful machines could be with us in ten to fifteen years time. However the problems to be solved are immense. Most things we want to use are made of trillions of atoms. It would take a long time to make anything useful one atom at a time. The first aim of nanotechnology is to produce a nanorobot that can make copies of itself. This robot could make copies and those copies could make copies. Soon billions of robots controlled by nano supercomputers would be assembling objects at great speed. There may be a gap of many years between the construction of the first assembler robot and the first 'miracle' products rolling off the microassembly line.

It is hoped that in the future robot insects will be able to perform repairs inside otherwise inaccessible machinery.

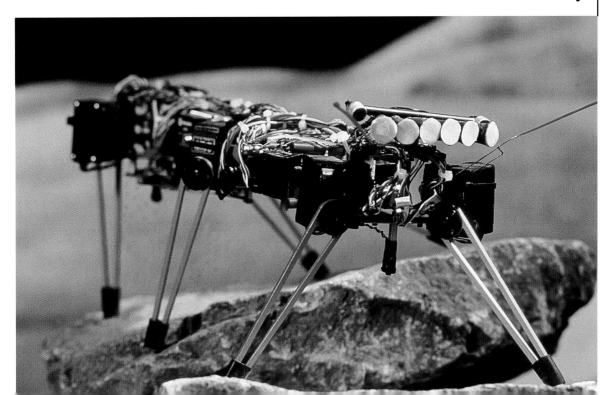

Glossary

alloy a mixture of two or more metals or a metal and a non-metal

antibiotic a substance produced by or obtained from certain bacteria or fungi that can be used to kill or inhibit the growth of disease-causing micro-organisms

asteroid one of a number of large rocky, metallic objects that orbit the sun; also called minor planets

atoms tiny particles from which all materials are made; the smallest part of an element that can exist

ceramics non-metallic solids that stay hard when heated

chemical plant factory where chemicals are produced on an industrial scale

compounds substances made up of atoms of two or more elements

conductors substances through which heat or electricity can be transmitted

corrosion the eating away of metals by chemicals; rusting is a type of corrosion

current a flow of something, such as a liquid, gas or electricity

durable not easily worn out

elements substances that cannot be broken down into simpler substances by chemical reactions; an element is made up of just one type of atom

extract to get out with difficulty or by force

fertilizers chemicals added to soil to provide nutrients for plant growth

fibres long threads of a material

furnace a chamber in which materials can be heated to a very high temperature

hazardous dangerous

insulators materials that block the flow of electricity or heat

minerals   naturally occurring solid substances; substances obtained by mining

molecule   two or more atoms combined together; if the atoms are the same it is an element, if they are different it is a compound

monomers   chemical compound composed of simple molecules from which polymers can be made by joining the monomers together

moulds   types of fungus

nutrients   substances that are essential for the maintenance of life

particles   tiny portions of matter

pesticides   chemicals used to kill insects and other pests that damage crops and livestock

polymers   long molecules formed by a chain of smaller molecules, called monomers, joined together

radiation   high energy rays or particles given off by radioactive atoms as they decay

raw materials   material in its natural state

refined   having had any impurities removed

resistance   the more energy it takes to get electricity to pass through a material the more resistance we say that material has

solution   a mixture of one substance dissolved in another

stress   a force acting on an object that changes its shape

superconductivity   the increase in a material's ability to conduct electricity at very low temperatures when its electrical resistance becomes practically zero

superconductors   materials that show superconductivity

voltage   units of electricity

Index